The Official
ENGLAND
Annual 2015

Written by Jon Culley

A Grange Publication

© 2014. Published by Grange Communications Ltd., Edinburgh, under licence from The Football Association. Printed in the EU.

Photography © Action Images

ISBN: 978-1-908925-65-7

£7.99

Contents

ROAD TO PARIS

England will appear in the Finals of the UEFA European Championship for the ninth time if they can negotiate a successful path through their Group E qualifying campaign and join 23 other teams when France host the 2016 Finals.

In the history of the tournament, England have been Semi-Finalists twice and Quarter-Finalists twice.

They lost to Yugoslavia in the Semi-Finals in Italy in 1968 and were beaten at the same stage by Germany on penalties when the Finals were staged in England in 1996. Although the record books show both achievements as equal, the circumstances were very different.

In 1968, only the top four teams from the 32-team qualification competition travelled to the Finals, having played the Quarter-Finals on a home-and-away basis.

In 1996, which is generally regarded as one of England's best performances in a tournament, there were 47 teams in the qualification competition of which 15 won through to join the hosts in the Finals.

To take their place automatically in France in 2016, England must finish in the top two of their six-team group or as the best third-placed team overall. Four other sides will qualify by finishing third and winning a play-off.

Read on for a closer look at England's five opponents in their qualifying group.

UEFA Fixtures...

Keep on top of England's Euro campaign by filling out the scores in the table below:

Euro 2016 Qualifying Fixtures		Score	
September 8, 2014	Switzerland (A)		
October 9, 2014	San Marino (H)		
October 12, 2014	Estonia (A)		
November 15, 2014	Slovenia (H)		
March 27, 2015	Lithuania (H)		
June 14, 2015	Slovenia (A)		
September 5, 2015	San Marino (A)		
September 8, 2015	Switzerland (H)		
October 9, 2015	Estonia (H)		
October 12, 2015	Lithuania (A)		

🇨🇭 SWITZERLAND

England will square off against a nation very familiar to manager Roy Hodgson when they do battle with the Swiss.

Hodgson was in charge of Switzerland between 1992 and 1995 and will be acutely aware that the country, famously neutral in foreign affairs, will be an especially difficult opponent for England en route to Euro 2016.

So impressive have the Swiss been lately that they were a surprise seed in the main draw of the World Cup in Brazil – ahead of England, amongst others – after an unbeaten qualification campaign.

Philippe Senderos and Johan Djourou are names Premier League fans will recognise but Switzerland's main stars lie in midfield, where the Napoli trio of Swiss captain Gokhan Inler, Valon Behrami and Blerim Dzemaili are joined by Bayern Munich's Xherdan Shaqiri.

England first met Switzerland in 1933, winning 4-0, and in recent times have encountered the Swiss twice in major tournaments, drawing 1-1 at Euro '96 and winning 3-0 at Euro 2004.

The countries last met in qualification for Euro 2012, drawing 2-2 at Wembley after Switzerland led 2-0, while England triumphed 3-1 in Basel through goals from Wayne Rooney, Adam Johnson and Darren Bent.

In England's favour, perhaps, going into this campaign is that the mastermind of Switzerland's recent success, ex-Bayern Munich manager Ottmar Hitzfeld, will no longer be at the helm, the German having retired after the World Cup to make way for Bosnian Vladimir Petkovic.

SAN MARINO

The record books say that no country in Europe need have any fears about taking on San Marino and Roy Hodgson's team should brush aside the tiny principality, having scored 13 times against them without reply in two qualifiers for the World Cup in Brazil.

In 25 years since first entering competitive international football, San Marino still boast no wins, their only success in any football coming in a 1-0 friendly win over Liechtenstein in 2004.

Such is their lowly status, a goal alone is worthy of a grand celebration. They have scored only 20 in their history, at a rate of less than one a year.

However, for England fans whose memories go back further than the 5-0 Wembley win in October 2012 and 8-0 thrashing away from home in March 2013, one of San Marino's goals still sends a shiver down the spine.

At Bologna's Stadio Renato dall'Ara – the host stadium because no Sammarinese venue was deemed capable of housing England's travelling fans – Davide Gualtieri scored after eight seconds, the fastest goal in World Cup history, when he pounced on an under-hit Stuart Pearce backpass.

England won the match 7-1 but for manager Graham Taylor the damage was symbolically done: they had to win by seven clear goals to stand any chance of reaching the 1994 World Cup Finals. In the event, results elsewhere rendered England's winning margin irrelevant anyway.

San Marino has produced only two players in the principality's history that have been good enough to play in Italy's Serie A. Their best-known current player is Andy Selva, still their captain at 38 and the country's record goalscorer with eight.

ESTONIA

Currently ranked 93rd by FIFA, Estonia cannot be described in the strictest sense as a minnow of international football but as a nation with ambitions to challenge for the title in Paris in 2016 England would hope to despatch them in relatively short order.

England's only two previous meetings with Estonia took place while Steve McClaren was in charge, both ending in convincing 3-0 wins.

The Baltic nation competed under its own name between 1918 and 1940, after which it was part of the Soviet Union until 1991.

Since the break-up of the USSR, Estonia have struggled to make a meaningful impression in international football, their greatest achievement to date coming in the qualification competition for Euro 2012, when they pipped Serbia to second place in their group, although they were soundly beaten in a play-off by Republic of Ireland.

Arguably Estonia's best player from their modest population of 1.3 million – roughly the same number that live in Kent – is midfielder Konstantin Vassiljev, who has 17 international goals to his name and plays for the Polish side, Piast Gliwice.

SLOVENIA

England would be wise not to write off the threat posed by Slovenia as the former Yugoslav nation have made a habit of springing surprises since returning to the international game under their own name in 1991.

The country, whose best known player is the Inter-Milan goalkeeper Samir Handanovic, has a population of only slightly more than two million.

They are always combative and have qualified for three major tournaments, most recently running England perilously close in the group stage of the 2010 World Cup, when a Jermain Defoe goal sealed a narrow win and a place in the knock-out stages.

The Slovenians were also the only nation to beat eventual winners Italy in the 2006 World Cup, triumphing 1-0 in Ljubljana in the qualifying stages.

This will be the first time England have squared up against Slovenia in qualification, although they did win a Wembley friendly 2-1 in 2009 in their only meeting on English soil.

Striker Milivoje Novakovic, who plays with Shimizu S-Pulse in Japan, retired from international football in 2012 but changed his mind a year later and returned to score a hat-trick against Norway in a World Cup 2014 qualifier.

🏴 LITHUANIA

Lithuania has thrived as a nation since breaking from the Soviet Union in 1990 but similar progress has yet to be made by its football team.

The largest of the three Baltic states with a population of three million, Lithuania's rapidly growing economy, its institutionalised democracy and a place on the UN Security Council reflect the giant strides made since gaining independence.

Their stock in European football is greater than that of a true minnow, but they have rarely threatened to mirror the shock achievement of neighbours Latvia, who qualified for Euro 2004. The closest they have come is two third-placed finishes in qualifying for Euro '96 and the France '98 World Cup.

England will be entering uncharted territory when they travel to Vilnius for their final qualifier in October 2015 as the countries have never previously met. They will be aware, though, that Lithuania have a reputation for surprising European giants, having drawn with Germany and Italy in the past.

Their most-capped player, defender Andrius Skerla, made many of his 84 international appearances while playing for Scottish club Dunfermline Athletic.

QUIZ TIME!
CROSSWORD

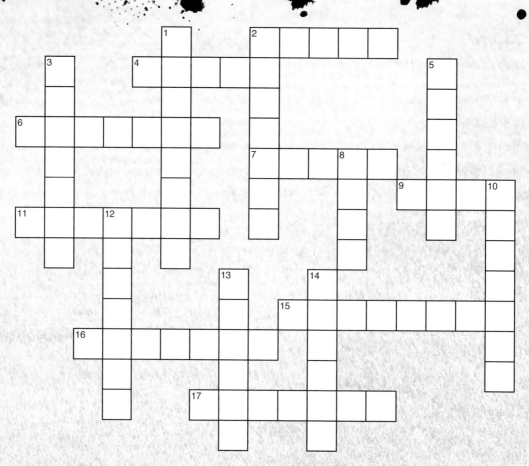

ACROSS

2   Colour of the England home strip. (5)

4   The number of goals scored in a hat trick. (5)

6   England were World Cup _____ in 1966. (7)

7   There are three of these on the England crest. (5)

9   The governing body of Association football. (4)

11   England's Manager. (7)

15   Current England women's team Captain. (8)

16   Vice-Captain of the England team at the 2014 World Cup. (7)

17   England's youngest ever player. (7)

DOWN

1   England's highest ever goal scorer. (8)

2   England's national stadium. (7)

3   He has played the most games for England at a World Cup. (7)

5   The country hosting the World Cup in 2018. (6)

8   Shirt sponsor. (4)

10   Hull City lost to this team in the FA Cup Final 2014. (7)

12   This player retired from international duty in 2014. (7)

13   England played this team in their first fixture of the 2014-15 season. (6)

14   England Manager at the World Cup Italia '90. (6)

Answers on Page 60

ENGLAND'S GREATEST GOALS #1

BOBBY CHARLTON
(2nd goal v Portugal, World Cup semi-final 1966)

England's only major tournament triumph is so long ago now that many fans have little or no recollection of it.

But, 49 years on from Bobby Moore receiving the Jules Rimet trophy from Her Majesty The Queen at Wembley, the contribution of another legend of that team, preserved in grainy TV footage, still occupies the thoughts of many wistful England fans.

Geoff Hurst's hat-trick goal in the Final against West Germany, to make the score 4-2, is the most iconic image of the tournament, yet without the contribution of Manchester United's Bobby Charlton, arguably the tournament's best player, England might not have got there.

In the semi-finals, England were pitted against Portugal and the mighty Eusebio, whose seven goals had swept his country passed the great Brazil and Hungary in the group stage.

Charlton was England's star attacking player and the July 26 semi-final at Wembley was billed by some as a duel between him and Eusebio. In the event it was two goals from Charlton against one from Eusebio that took England to the Final.

The United man put England ahead in the first half, capitalising on the Portuguese goalkeeper spilling a shot but England's mean defence, who had not conceded a single goal on the way to the last four, came under increasing pressure from Eusebio and company.

But with ten minutes to go, Charlton lifted the tension around Wembley with a typically thunderous strike.

Moore distributed the ball to full-back George Cohen in his own half. Cohen's lofted pass down the right found Hurst who held the ball up and slotted it perfectly into the path of the advancing Charlton, who slammed his shot into the right corner.

Eusebio scored a few minutes later – his eighth of the competition – from the penalty spot after Charlton's brother Jack handled, but England held on to set up their landmark triumph against the Germans on 30 July.

Winning the World Cup meant a great deal to every Englishman, but none more so than Charlton, who had overcome huge emotional turmoil to become England's best player, eight years after walking away uninjured from the Munich air disaster, which claimed the lives of eight of his teammates among 15 other people.

BRAZIL 2014

GROUP A

Brazil 3 Croatia 1	
Mexico 1 Cameroon 0	
Brazil 0 Mexico 0	
Cameroon 0 Croatia 4	
Cameroon 1 Brazil 4	
Croatia 1 Mexico 3	

Qualified:
Brazil & Mexico

Eliminated:
Croatia & Cameroon

GROUP B

Spain 1 Netherlands 5	
Chile 3 Australia 1	
Spain 0 Chile 2	
Australia 2 Netherlands 3	
Australia 0 Spain 3	
Netherlands 2 Chile 0	

Qualified:
Netherlands & Chile

Eliminated:
Spain & Australia

GROUP C

Colombia 3 Greece 0	
Ivory Coast 2 Japan 1	
Colombia 2 Ivory Coast 1	
Japan 0 Greece 0	
Greece 2 Ivory Coast 1	
Japan 1 Colombia 4	

Qualified:
Colombia & Greece

Eliminated:
Japan & Ivory Coast

GROUP D

Uruguay 1 Costa Rica 3	
England 1 Italy 2	
Uruguay 2 England 1	
Italy 0 Costa Rica 1	
Costa Rica 0 England 0	
Italy 0 Uruguay 1	

Qualified:
Costa Rica & Uruguay

Eliminated:
England & Italy

GROUP E

Switzerland 2 Ecuador 1	
France 3 Honduras 0	
Switzerland 2 France 5	
Honduras 1 Ecuador 2	
Ecuador 0 France 0	
Honduras 0 Switzerland 3	

Qualified:
France & Switzerland

Eliminated:
Ecuador & Honduras

GROUP F

Argentina 2 Bosnia-Herzegovina 1	
Iran 0 Nigeria 0	
Argentina 1 Iran 0	
Nigeria 1 Bosnia-Herzegovina 0	
Bosnia-Herzegovina 3 Iran 1	
Nigeria 2 Argentina 3	

Qualified:
Argentina & Nigeria

Eliminated:
Bosnia-Herzegovina & Iran

GROUP G

Germany 4 Portugal 0	
Ghana 1 USA 2	
Germany 2 Ghana 2	
USA 2 Portugal 2	
Portugal 2 Ghana 1	
USA 0 Germany 1	

Qualified:
Germany & USA

Eliminated:
Portugal & Ghana

GROUP H

Belgium 2 Algeria 1	
Russia 1 South Korea 1	
Belgium 1 Russia 0	
South Korea 2 Algeria 4	
Algeria 1 Russia 1	
South Korea 0 Belgium 1	

Qualified:
Belgium & Algeria

Eliminated:
Russia & South Korea

ENGLAND: The World Cup Verdict

England produced some encouraging performances at Brazil 2014 even though they were unable to progress beyond the group stage.

In that respect they matched what happened at the last World Cup to be staged in Brazil in 1950, when England's results included a 1-0 defeat in Belo Horizonte to a United States team fielding many part-time players, which remains one of the biggest upsets in the tournament's history.

This time, 64 years on, England bowed out with a 0-0 draw against Costa Rica in the same city, but although the team came home without a win there were reasons to be optimistic about the national side's future prospects."

Roy Hodgson boldly picked a squad that showcased many of the talented young players who had shone over the preceding 12 months in the Premier League, which meant that some more experienced heads such as Michael Carrick and Ashley Cole missed out.

England were presented with a tough group, pitted against two fellow previous winners in Italy and Uruguay. Defeats to both spelt the end for Hodgson's men while the eventual group winners, the relatively unheralded Costa Rica, were a far cry from the novices from America that stunned Walter Winterbottom's England on their World Cup debut in 1950.

Inexperience and a lack of know-how ultimately cost England but neither shortcoming is a long-term one. And even in defeat against Italy and Uruguay, Hodgson's team still played with a vibrancy and freedom lacking in South Africa four years previously.

It could be argued that England should have beaten Italy and might easily have won against Uruguay. Ultimately, it took world class performers in Andrea Pirlo and Mario Balotelli for Italy and Luis Suarez for Uruguay to provide the moments that decided those matches.

But there was enough evidence across England's three matches to suggest that some youngsters in their ranks can one day scale similar heights and become players for the big moments.

Despite the outcome, Ross Barkley, Raheem Sterling and Daniel Sturridge will have benefited from their involvement in a major tournament, as will Alex Oxlade-Chamberlain, even though injury deprived him of an appearance.

Some stellar names from England's past -- Steven Gerrard for one – will not be at the Finals in Russia in 2018, but the far-sightedness with which Hodgson selected his squad for Brazil means England can build a new, street-wise group with tournament experience behind them and again be a threat in the knock-out stages.

England 1 Italy 2

Saturday June 14, 2014; Arena de Amazonia, Manaus.

Goals: Marchisio (35) 0-1; Sturridge (37) 1-1; Balotelli (50) 1-2.

England gained plaudits but no points from their opening World Cup match with Italy in the humid surroundings of the Amazon rainforest.

There were fears that the sticky climate of Manaus could hinder England, but a dynamic attacking performance, spearheaded by Liverpool's Raheem Sterling, dispelled such worries, although ultimately it was the Italians, conquerors of England in the Quarter-Finals of Euro 2012, who triumphed.

England fans were brought to their feet in the opening minutes when Sterling unleashed a stinging drive from 25 yards, the attacking midfielder's drive crashing into the side netting at such an angle it seemed to have gone in. A 1-0 scoreline even appeared on TV screens momentarily.

But alongside England's enterprising ambition going forward were intermittent signs of defensive vulnerability.

A clever dummy from Andrea Pirlo, the chief orchestrator of Italy's attacking threat, made the opening goal. He deceived Daniel Sturridge by feigning to control the ball from a corner, creating acres of space for Claudio Marchisio to place a shot past Joe Hart into the bottom corner.

England were behind for just two minutes as a quick counter saw Wayne Rooney, deployed on the left side of midfield, pick out Sturridge with a perfectly weighted pass to tap in.

Antonio Candreva nearly restored Italy's lead before half-time when his shot hit the woodwork but Mario Balotelli was less forgiving on the hour mark when he escaped the attentions of Gary Cahill to head in Italy's second.

England rallied, Rooney dragging arguably their best chance of an equaliser wide. Pirlo then rattled the bar with a swerving free-kick in the closing stages as England lost their opening game for the first time since 1986.

TEAMS

England (4-2-3-1):

Hart; Johnson, Cahill, Jagielka, Baines; Gerrard, Henderson (Wilshere 73); Sterling, Welbeck (Barkley 61), Rooney; Sturridge (Lallana 80).

Yellow card: Sterling.

Italy (4-3-3):

Sirigu; Darmian, Paletta, Barzagli, Chiellini; Verratti (Motta 57), Pirlo, De Rossi; Candreva (Parolo 79), Balotelli (Immobile 73), Marchisio.

Uruguay 2 **England 1**

Thursday June 19, 2014; Arena de Sao Paulo, Sao Paulo.

Goals: Suarez (39) 1-0; Rooney (75) 1-1; Suarez (85) 2-1.

Luis Suarez returned from injury to haunt his Liverpool colleagues in the England team and leave Roy Hodgson's men on the brink of a group stage exit.

Back in action following knee surgery, Suarez gave Uruguay the lead when he escaped the attention of Phil Jagielka to head past Joe Hart and later capitalised on a misplaced header from club teammate Steven Gerrard to secure victory.

England were less fluent than they had been against Italy but when Wayne Rooney equalised with 15 minutes to go they seemed set to push for victory.

Rooney returned to the number 10 role and was England's greatest threat in the first half, curling a free-kick wide and cannoning a header against the bar from two yards out.

Uruguay, well beaten by Costa Rica in their opening match, seemed to have little to offer but in Suarez and Edinson Cavani they had two men capable of hurting England.

And so it proved as Cavani picked out Suarez with a perfect cross six minutes before half-time after England had surrendered possession in midfield.

No team had ever progressed from the group stage after losing their first two matches, so England knew they could ill afford defeat but salvation beckoned when Liverpool right-back Glen Johnson supplied Rooney with an easy finish after slotting a cross across the six-yard box.

It was Suarez who would have the last laugh, though, slamming a shot past Hart five minutes from time to leave England needing a miracle.

Down and very nearly out, England required Italy to beat both Costa Rica and Uruguay and to achieve a convincing win of their own against a surprisingly impressive Costa Rica in their final game.

TEAMS

Uruguay (4-3-1-2):

Muslera; Caceres, Gimenez, Godin, Pereira; Gonzales (Fucile 78), Arevalo Rios, Rodriguez; Lodeiro (Stuani 67); Cavani, Suarez (Coates 88).

Yellow card: Godin.

England (4-2-3-1):

Hart; Johnson, Cahill, Jagielka, Baines; Gerrard, Henderson (Lambert 87); Sterling (Barkley 64), Rooney, Welbeck (Lallana 71); Sturridge.

Yellow card: Gerrard.

Costa Rica 0 **England 0**

Tuesday June 24, 2014; Mineirao, Belo Horizonte.

England were unable to break down a stubborn Costa Rica side as they bowed out of the World Cup without a victory.

Roy Hodgson made several changes, with elimination already confirmed after Costa Rica beat Italy, with Frank Lampard captaining the side in place of Steven Gerrard.

Daniel Sturridge went closest for England but spurned several chances as England were forced to endure the disappointment of finishing bottom of the group. Their opponents cemented their surprise impact in the competition by taking a point to finish top.

England's back-up goalkeeper Ben Foster was forced into a stunning save by a Celso Borges free-kick in the first half.

Liverpool's Sturridge went close four times, heading over and firing a shot from distance wide in the first half. Then, after the break, his control let him down as he allowed goalkeeper Keylor Navas time to leap from his line and smother his effort.

Jack Wilshere found him inside the box with a clever flick late on but his finish arrowed past the bottom corner. Gerrard and Wayne Rooney made late bows from the bench, with the latter's crafty chip almost deceiving Navas, but both were ultimately powerless to prevent a drab stalemate.

TEAMS

Costa Rica (5-4-1):

Navas; Gamboa, Duarte, Gonzalez, Miller, Diaz; Ruiz, Borges (Barrantes 78), Tejeda, Brenes (Bolanos 59); Campbell (Urena 65).

Yellow card: Gonzalez.

England (4-2-3-1):

Foster; Jones, Smalling, Cahill, Shaw; Lampard, Wilshere (Gerrard 73); Milner (Rooney 76), Barkley, Lallana (Sterling 62); Sturridge.

Yellow cards: Barkley, Lallana.

Germany ended their 24 year wait to win a fourth World Cup by becoming the first country from Europe to become champions in South America.

Their team of talented young players, pulled together by the experience of the combative Bastian Schweinsteiger and the inspirational Philipp Lahm and led in attack by the brilliant Thomas Muller, swept aside all before them and dispelled the pain of narrowly missing out on the top prize in the last three major tournaments, with one of the new generation, 22-year-old, Mario Gotze, providing the winning goal in the Final.

Striker Miroslav Klose became the leading World Cup goalscorer of all time although Muller, only 25, could well overhaul his total of 16, having already netted 10.

In the early part of the tournament, the European nations suffered major casualties as Italy, reigning champions Spain and Cristiano Ronaldo's Portugal joined England in exiting at the group stage.

The Spanish experience was especially painful, beginning with a humbling 5-1 loss as The Netherlands exacted sweet revenge for their defeat in the Final in South Africa in 2010.

The Dutch never hit the same heights again, stumbling past Mexico in their last 16 match and needing penalties to beat Costa Rica in the quarter-finals before running out of luck in the semi-finals, when Argentina prevailed in another shoot-out.

Among the South American sides, Colombia had wowed fans in breezing to the quarter-finals, Monaco's James Rodriguez bursting onto the world stage by scoring six goals to win the Golden Boot. They were edged out by Brazil, although not before they had beaten Uruguay, by then without Luis Suarez, who was starting his four-month ban for sensationally biting Italy defender Giorgio Chiellini.

Brazil's visions of winning their own tournament were ended dramatically when they met Germany in the semi-finals, which produced one of the most astounding results in World Cup history. With the tournament's poster boy, Neymar, injured and captain Thiago Silva banned, Brazil suffered a 7-1 humiliation that was seen as a national disaster.

Argentina's hopes in the Final rested on Barcelona's brilliant forward, Lionel Messi, who had at times seemed almost to be dragging his country through. How he would have loved to match Diego Maradona, his legendary predecessor in the number 10 shirt, by winning the World Cup for his country. Germany put a stop to this dream.

Six years ago, Germany won the 2009 European Under-21 Championship, beating England 4-0 in the Final with a team containing Manuel Neuer, Mezut Ozil, Sami Khedira, Benedikt Howedes, Mats Hummels and Jerome Boateng, all key figures last summer.

It was a major step on a road to redemption for Germany that began after the shock of losing in the group stages of Euro 2000, after which the German FA travelled the world to find ways to improve their system. Winning in Brazil was the reward.

GOALKEEPERS

Fraser **Forster**

Born: Hexham, Northumberland, 17 March, 1988

Fraser Forster earned a berth in Roy Hodgson's World Cup squad in 2014 as the only member of the party never to have made an appearance in the English Premier League.

However, the former Celtic keeper, who joined Southampton last summer, had already proved his ability on the world stage for the Glasgow club, keeping Lionel Messi and Barcelona at bay in the Champions League in a famous Parkhead victory in 2012.

His stock has risen to such heights that most England fans would probably regard Forster as Joe Hart's main understudy.

Born in the north-east, Forster came through the youth ranks at Newcastle United but despite being on their senior books for six years up to being released in 2012, he never made a first-team appearance.

He first attracted attention in a loan spell at Norwich City, where he helped the Norfolk club to the 2009-10 League One title, before his career took off during a loan spell at Celtic which turned into a permanent move.

DID YOU KNOW?

Fraser is now a giant presence at 6ft 7in tall, yet coaches once feared he would not be tall enough to be a goalkeeper, until a growth spurt when he was 15 prompted Newcastle United to recruit him from Wallsend Boys Club.

Ben **Foster**

Born: Leamington Spa, Warwickshire, 3 April, 1983

Having returned to the fore after a self-imposed break from England duty, Ben Foster is keen to build on a period of stability in his career at current club West Bromwich Albion and challenge Joe Hart's position as England's number one.

When Foster adopted a watching brief from the bench as England brushed aside minnows San Marino 8-0 in March 2013, it was his first involvement in an England squad for over two years.

If the break has given his career a boost, then so too has the chance to enjoy permanent surroundings. He has been at the Hawthorns for more than three years, having previously spent more than half of his career out on loan from his former clubs.

Foster won his first cap – having never represented his country at any age group – against Spain in 2007 and he was on Sven Goran Eriksson's reserve list for the 2006 World Cup at the age of just 23.

Foster began his senior career at Stoke before his youthful promise won him a move to Manchester United, but he was largely second or third choice in his three-year stay at Old Trafford. He established his reputation during a loan spell at Watford, helping the Hornets win promotion to the Premier League in 2006, before he moved to Birmingham City in 2010, helping them to their first major trophy in 48 years when they won the 2011 Carling Cup.

DID YOU KNOW?

Ben won his sixth England cap against Republic of Ireland at Wembley in May 2013, 923 days after he won his fifth, in a defeat to France, at the same venue.

Joe **Hart**

Born: Shrewsbury, Shropshire, 19 April, 1987

A Premier League champion for the second time last season, Joe Hart recovered from a difficult period early in the campaign to help Manchester City to the title and confirm his status as one of the best goalkeepers in world football.

England's number one choice since the aftermath of the 2010 World Cup, Hart got his first taste of international tournament football at Euro 2012 although he could do nothing to stop England losing a Quarter-Final penalty shoot-out to Italy.

Hart has won all the major domestic honours at City, having made the momentous move to the Etihad Stadium in 2006, direct from hometown club Shrewsbury Town, where he started his career.

The Shropshire-born player gained many plaudits during a loan spell at Birmingham City, where he helped them to their best Premier League finish before returning to his parent club in 2010.

After making his senior debut against Trinidad and Tobago in a friendly in Port of Spain in June 2008, he was first choice keeper for England's Under-21s at Euro 2009, saving a penalty in a shoot-out Semi-Final win over Sweden in which he also scored one of England's penalties. Hart won his 40th cap against Peru at Wembley in England's first World Cup warm-up match.

DID YOU KNOW?

England's 2-1 loss to Italy at the 2014 World Cup was the first competitive defeat in normal time in Joe's international career.

ENGLAND TRIVIA

Gary Lineker scored the 42nd of his 48 England goals in the 42nd second of a friendly against Malaysia in Kuala Lumpur in June 1991.

Manager Ron Greenwood gave the England captain's armband to seven different players in two seasons between 1980 and 1982.

Of the 2014 World Cup Finalists, England have never played an international fixture against Bosnia and Herzegovina, Iran or Ivory Coast.

Jermain Defoe has scored more goals -- seven -- as a substitute than any other England player.

Roy Hodgson is the eighth different England manager to select midfielder Gareth Barry, who made his debut in 2000 under Kevin Keegan.

Stan Mortensen, the Blackpool centre-forward who won 25 England caps between 1947 and 1953, made his international debut as a guest player for Wales in a 1944 wartime match.

Theo Walcott took Wayne Rooney's record as England's youngest ever player on 30 May, 2006 when he came on as a 65th-minute substitute against Hungary at Old Trafford, aged 17 years and 75 days old. But Rooney remains the youngest player to start for England, aged 17 years and 160 days when he lined up against Turkey on April 2, 2003.

The selection of Luke Shaw, Adam Lallana and Rickie Lambert in Roy Hodgson's squad for the 2014 World Cup Finals was the first time Southampton had provided three players in an England squad since January 1986, when Peter Shilton, Danny Wallace and Mark Wright all played in a 4-0 win over Egypt.

Bryan Robson, famous for scoring England's fastest goal in a competitive match after 27 seconds against France in the 1982 World Cup Finals, scored inside the first minute for England on two other occasions, after 38 seconds of a friendly against Yugoslavia in 1989 and after 44 seconds of a Home International against Northern Ireland in 1982.

Frank Lampard is England's record scorer of penalties with nine goals from the spot but he also missed two, against Hungary at Old Trafford in 2006 and against Japan in Austria in 2010.

QUIZ TIME!
MAZE

Use your expert dribbling skills to manouvre the ball out from the centre of the maze.

Answer on Page 60

ENGLAND'S GREATEST GOALS #2

DAVID PLATT
(v Belgium, World Cup Italia 1990, round of 16)

The glitz and glamour of the Barclays FA Premier League has turned football into a consumer product enjoying almost universal popularity. Stadiums are now the domain of families and children as much as the place for traditional fans to congregate and roar on their teams.

Going into the Italia '90 World Cup Finals, however, things were very different. Hooliganism was rife and the reputation of England and their teams in Europe was at its lowest.

The Heysel Stadium Disaster in 1985, when 39 people, mostly Juventus fans, were killed at the European Cup Final between the Italian club and Liverpool, led to English clubs being banned from European competition for six years.

In Italia '90, England played their group matches on the island of Sardinia but while they progressed to the second phase they had failed to impress. They returned to the Italian mainland for their last-16 clash with Belgium but struggled through a poor match that was goalless after 90 minutes.

But, with penalties looming in the 29th minute of extra time, Paul Gascoigne and David Platt combined to take England to the last eight in a truly jaw-dropping moment.

England won a free-kick on the left. Gascoigne showed his instinctive football intelligence by taking it quickly after spotting Platt free at the back post, but it was the brilliance of the then Aston Villa midfielder that took the breath away.

Gascoigne's lofted ball into the area went over his teammate's shoulder but, watching it all the way as it came down, Platt swivelled and scored with a stunning volley to send England through.

It would not be true to say that Platt's goal revitalised football in England. The influx of foreign stars as the new Premier League sparked a globalisation of the English game had much to do with that.

But after England had gone on to beat Cameroon in the last eight, an estimated 26.2m viewers tuned in at home to watch their semi-final against West Germany, many sharing Gascoigne's tears as his booking ruled him out of playing in the Final, before the heartbreak of defeat on penalties had the whole team bemoaning their fate.

England's performance at Italia '90 re-engaged the masses with the national obsession. Yet none of it would have happened without Platt's fabulous strike against Belgium in Bologna.

England's Football
Firsts...

The first player to score a goal for England was **William Kenyon-Slaney**, who found the net after two minutes of England's match against Scotland on 8 March, 1873. It was England's second official international match. The first – also against Scotland, in 1972 – ended in a goalless draw. Kenyon-Slaney, who played as a forward for Wanderers, was educated at Eton and went on to be a Colonel in the Grenadier Guards as well as a Conservative MP.

Henry Cursham, a forward with Notts County, scored the first hat-trick by an England player in a competitive match in an 8-1 win over Ireland in Belfast on 23 February, 1884, in the British Home Championship. Cursham, who also played first-class cricket for Nottinghamshire, still holds the record for the most FA Cup goals by a single player, having scored 49 between 1877 and 1887.

On 18 February, 1899, **Jimmy Crabtree**, the Aston Villa half-back, became the first England player to take a penalty against Ireland in the British Home Championship at Roker Park in Sunderland on 18 February 1899. He missed, although it hardly mattered: England won 13-2.

Legendary Newcastle United centre-forward **Jackie Milburn** became the first England player to be substituted when he was injured after 10 minutes of England's friendly against Belgium in Brussels on 18 May, 1950, manager Walter Winterbottom replacing him with Jimmy Mullen, of Wolves.

(Statue commemorating Billy Wright, first England player to win 100 caps)

On 11 April, 1959 captain **Billy Wright** became the first England player to win 100 caps when he lined up against Scotland at Wembley. England won 1-0 thanks to a goal by Bobby Charlton but it was Wolves defender Wright who received the applause, carried off the field on the shoulders of teammates Don Howe and Ronnie Clayton.

Jimmy Greaves, the Tottenham forward, became the first England player to score five hat-tricks when England beat Northern Ireland 4-3 in Belfast on 3 October, 1964. He added a sixth in a 6-1 drubbing of Norway in Oslo in June 1966 in a warm-up match ahead of the World Cup Finals.

On 5 June, 1968 in Florence, England played a European Championship Semi-Final against Yugoslavia which turned into a notably bruising encounter. Several England players felt the ferocity of the Yugoslav tackling, which became too much for Tottenham midfielder **Alan Mullery**, whose retaliatory kick at an opponent in the dying moments of a 1-0 defeat made him the first England player to be sent off.

After Kevin Keegan resigned in October 2000, England put former England Under-21 coach Peter Taylor in charge for one match but then moved to appoint the Swede **Sven-Goran Eriksson**, who had enjoyed considerable success in domestic football in Sweden, Portugal and Italy, as the first non-Englishman to manage the England team.

DEFENDERS

Leighton **Baines**

Born: Kirkby, Merseyside, 11 December, 1984

Few first choice England players are more deserving of their status than Everton's Leighton Baines who, now Ashley Cole has retired from international football, has established the left-back position as his own as well as earning recognition as one of the team's set-piece specialists.

Liverpool-born and a Liverpool supporter as a boy, Baines joined Everton from Wigan in 2007, after being an integral member of the Latics team which rose from the lower leagues to the top flight, winning the Division Two title in his first full season and helping seal promotion to the Premier League in 2005.

After reaching the 2006 Carling Cup Final with Wigan, Baines secured a £5m move to Goodison Park, where his consistently high-quality performances have helped Everton finish no lower than eighth place in each of his seven seasons with the club and earn a trip to Wembley for the 2009 FA Cup Final.

Capped 16 times at Under-21 level, Baines was unlucky to miss the 2010 World Cup but was included in Roy Hodgson's 23-man squad at Euro 2012. He was a fixture in the side at the Finals in Brazil last summer, four years after he won his first cap against Egypt at Wembley.

Not only a safe bet from 12 yards as Everton's regular penalty taker, Baines is capable of delivering devastating quality from free-kicks, winning Everton's 2011 'Goal of the Season' award, but he had scored only once in an England shirt ahead of the World Cup last summer.

DID YOU KNOW?

A huge music fan, Leighton is a good friend of Miles Kane, former frontman of The Rascals, and has accompanied him to several gigs and Glastonbury.

Gary **Cahill**

Born: Dronfield, Derbyshire, 19 December, 1985

Gary Cahill's club career took a couple of turns before he established himself as a top-class defender but he has since turned himself into England's leading centre-half.

Cahill earned himself a place in Villa folklore when his extraordinary bicycle-kick in the second city derby against Birmingham brought him his only goal for the club in 2006 but was sold to Bolton Wanderers in 2008, having been on loan at Sheffield United.

Cahill developed into a reliable, top-class defender at what is now the Macron Stadium, making 147 appearances for Wanderers and ensuring the club retained Premier League status for four straight seasons. His form at Bolton earned him an England call-up against Bulgaria at Wembley in 2010. He scored his first international goal against the same opposition the following year.

The 6ft 2in defender was promptly recruited by Andre Villas-Boas to Chelsea, where he has won Champions League, Europa League and FA Cup winners' medals and won the approval of Jose Mourinho on his return to Stamford Bridge, the Portuguese coach handing Cahill 47 appearances in the 2013-14 season.

Cahill represented his country at Under-20 and Under-21 levels and only injury deprived him of a place in Roy Hodgson's 23-man squad at Euro 2012. A first choice at the World Cup in Brazil, Cahill has an impressive goal-scoring record for a centre-half and struck his second in international football against Holland in 2012.

DID YOU KNOW?

Gary is one of three members of the 2014 England World Cup squad to have played for Bolton Wanderers, the others being Daniel Sturridge and Jack Wilshere, who had loan spells at the club.

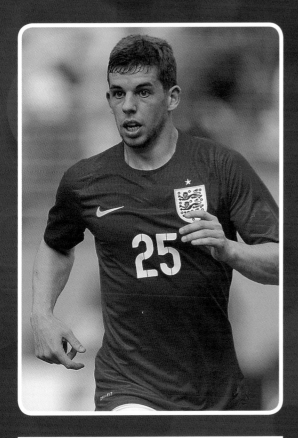

Jon **Flanagan**

Born: Liverpool, 1 January, 1993

The latest home-grown product of Liverpool's academy, Jon Flanagan was an understated but integral part of the team that went close to taking the title to Anfield for the first time in 24 years when they were narrow runners-up to Manchester City in 2013-14.

Flanagan only made his England senior debut against Ecuador in a World Cup warm-up in Miami but Roy Hodgson had been so impressed by his form for Liverpool he was willing to overlook his lack of international experience to include him on the standby list for the tournament in Brazil.

Kenny Dalglish gave Flanagan his first opportunity to impress at Anfield in 2011, when he helped the Reds beat Manchester City 3-0 at the age of 18.

Injuries during the 2012-13 season disrupted his progress, but he became a regular at left-back under Brendan Rodgers the following year, and scored his first goal for Liverpool from long range in a memorable 5-0 win away at Tottenham.

After making appearances for England's under-19s and under-21s, there were reports that Flanagan's Irish grandparents were encouraging Martin O'Neill to persuade the Liverpudlian to represent Republic of Ireland at senior level, but he has now committed to the Three Lions.

DID YOU KNOW?

Jon has won a host of admirers in his short career but none more qualified to comment than legendary Brazilian right-back Cafu, who said in May last year that he saw shades of his own playing style in the Liverpool man.

Phil **Jagielka**

Born: Sale, Greater Manchester, 17 August, 1982

Phil Jagielka is another player whose impressive form for Everton has been the platform for a rapid rise in the England ranks but the dependable central defender has always looked comfortable with his status as one of England's first-choice centre backs.

If Roberto Martinez's impressive first season as Everton manager had been capped with a top-four finish then Jagielka, now in his 30s, would have jumped at the chance to test himself at the highest level of club football.

Blessed with excellent aerial ability, Jagielka is also adept with the ball at his feet, having initially played as a midfielder under Neil Warnock at Sheffield United, before he left the Blades in a £4m move to Everton in 2007. Exceptionally versatile, he even played in goal at Bramall Lane, where Warnock had such faith in Jagielka's ability to step in he rarely named a replacement 'keeper among his substitutes.

Jagielka helped the Toffees to the 2009 FA Cup Final, scoring the winning penalty against Manchester United in the Semi-Final, and was Everton's 'Player of the Year' in the same season.

He was forced to wait until he was nearly 26 to win his first senior cap, which Fabio Capello handed him in a friendly against Trinidad & Tobago in 2008, but more opportunities in international football surely beckon for Jagielka, who scored his first England goal in a 2012 friendly with Italy in Berne.

DID YOU KNOW?

Because he has a Polish grandfather, Nikodem, from whom he takes his middle name, Phil could have opted to represent Poland.

Luke **Shaw**

Born: Kingston-upon-Thames, London, 12 July, 1995

Teenage left-back Luke Shaw is so highly regarded that Roy Hodgson picked him for his 23-man squad for the 2014 World Cup ahead of Ashley Cole, who is an all-time great among England defenders and Shaw's idol.

Shaw's rise has been spectacular. In Southampton's 2011-12 Championship winning campaign, he did not make a single appearance, yet he was virtually an ever-present two years later as manager Mauricio Pochettino guided the Saints to an eighth-placed Premier League finish.

His £30 million transfer to Manchester United last summer made him football's most expensive teenager, the fee beating the £25.6 million United paid for Wayne Rooney in 2004 as the world record for a player under 20 years old.

Shaw made his first team debut for Southampton aged 16 in an FA Cup tie with Millwall in 2012.

At just 18 he was selected in the PFA's 2013-14 Team of the Year and also was shortlisted for the Young Player of the Year award.

Like many teenage prodigies before him, Shaw did not spend long playing in the England Under-21 side, making three appearances before he was called up to the senior squad, winning his first cap against Denmark in a Wembley friendly in March last year.

DID YOU KNOW?

A Chelsea fan as a child, Shaw attended Chelsea's development centre in Guildford but took up an offer to join Southampton's academy when he was eight years old.

Chris **Smalling**

Born: Greenwich, London, 22 November, 1989

Chris Smalling was a keen member of Roy Hodgson's 23-man squad for the World Cup in Brazil last summer after injury robbed him of the chance to shine at Euro 2012.

A double Premier League champion, Smalling will hope to stay injury-free and thrive at Manchester United under the stewardship of Louis Van Gaal, while challenging Gary Cahill and Phil Jagielka for a place in the centre of England's defence.

The Londoner is as adept at right-back as in the middle of the back four and this versatility persuaded Manchester United to pay Fulham £8m for his services in 2010. He made only 13 first-team appearances for Fulham, but has grown in stature since moving to Old Trafford despite a succession of injury frustrations, scoring his first league goal for the club against Chelsea in 2011.

In three seasons at United, the defender has scooped two Premier League titles and been a Champions League runner-up – when United lost to Barcelona in 2011 – which works well for his future prospects.

Smalling made his senior England bow against Bulgaria in 2011 and travelled to Brazil having never lost a competitive international match. He was capped 14 times at under-21 level, scoring the winning goal against Romania in a European Championship play-off in 2010.

DID YOU KNOW?

Smalling won the first trophy of his senior career on his debut for Manchester United against Chelsea in the 2010 Community Shield.

John **Stones**

Born: Barnsley, 28 May, 1994

John Stones went from being a Championship centre-half to winning his first England caps in less than 18 months, and he will look to win a place in the main squad should England reach Euro 2016 after he was named as cover for last summer's World Cup.

Stones made only 28 appearances for home town club Barnsley, but he impressed sufficiently in South Yorkshire to prompt David Moyes to recruit him during the 2013 January transfer window.

Roberto Martinez underlined his faith in young players by making Stones a regular in the Everton side after he made his first Premier League start against Stoke on New Year's Day 2014.

A player who can also operate at right-back, Stones was recruited to England's squad in preparation for the Finals in Brazil when Phil Jones suffered a shoulder injury and he won his caps, both as a substitute, against Peru and Ecuador in the run-in to the tournament. He has been a regular for the under-21s having previously represented England at under-19 and under-20 level.

At Barnsley, he made his senior debut aged only 17 against Reading in March, 2012, and scored his first senior goal against Rochdale in a League Cup tie.

DID YOU KNOW?

John's signing was the last of 257 player transactions that took place during the 11 years in which David Moyes was Everton manager, including loan moves.

Kyle **Walker**

Born: Sheffield, 28 May, 1990

Blessed with electric pace, right-back Kyle Walker may think he is cursed after injury ruled him out of both Euro 2012 and last summer's World Cup. But the Tottenham man should be confident that more opportunities will be forthcoming after forcing himself into Spurs' first choice team in 2011 following an impressive loan spell at Aston Villa.

The Yorkshire-born defender began his career at Sheffield United, where his pace and talent prompted Spurs to sign him after making only seven appearances for the Blades, one of which was the 2009 Championship play-off Final at Wembley.

His efforts in the 2011-12 season earned him the PFA's 'Young Player of the Year Award' and international recognition. Of particular delight to Spurs fans was the manner of his first goal for the club – a 30-yard screamer against arch-rivals Arsenal.

Walker was England's starting right-back for the World Cup matches with Moldova, Ukraine and Montenegro in the autumn of 2013, helping them accrue seven vital points on the way to the Finals in Brazil.

Suspension ruled him out of the Final qualifier with Poland, though, and he has had to bide his time to reclaim a regular berth since, because of injury. Walker played for the Under-19 and Under-21 teams and was named in the 'Team of the Tournament' for the 2011 European Championships. He made his first senior start against Sweden at Wembley in November 2011.

DID YOU KNOW?

Back in the day: 1965

I f the retirement of Sir Stanley Matthews in February 1965 – six days after his 50th birthday – confirmed the passing of one era, the evolution of the England team under the later-to-be-knighted Alf Ramsey signalled the beginning of another.

This was the year that Ramsey began to experiment with the 4-3-3 formation that would prove the bedrock of England's success in the 1966 World Cup Finals, certainly in the group stage.

He tried it for the first time in a friendly against West Germany in Nuremberg in May, which England won 1-0, and again against Spain in Madrid in December, where a resounding 2-0 victory convinced Ramsey that it would be the basis of his tactics at the World Cup. A dubious press were slightly mocking of his 'wingless wonders' but Ramsey was never one to be swayed by such criticism.

Ramsey's jigsaw began to fall into place in terms of personnel, too. Nobby Stiles, who would be the defensive midfielder in the 4-1-3-2 system deployed in the Final in 1966, made his debut against Scotland in May, which also saw Jack Charlton, the Leeds centre half, appear for the first time. He and Bobby were the first brothers to play together in an England team since the previous century.

England drew 2-2 with Scotland but won the Home Championship and then embarked on a three-match summer tour that saw Alan Ball introduced in midfield in a 1-1 draw against Yugoslavia in Belgrade before beating the Germans in Nuremberg and winning against Sweden in Gothenburg.

A goalless draw against Wales and a 3-2 defeat by Austria at Wembley in October brought Ramsey's conviction that England would win the World Cup under scrutiny but the win in Madrid ended the year on a high note, the game also significant for a fine goal by Roger Hunt, the Liverpool striker, whose performance in the absence of Jimmy Greaves, who was out of action through illness, was another influence on Ramsey's thinking in 1966.

Roger Hunt

Bobby and Jack Charlton

Jack Charlton

Alf Ramsey and Bobby Moore

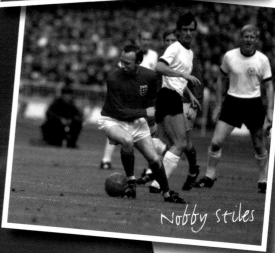

Nobby Stiles

QUIZ TIME!
GUESS WHO?

Can you guess who the current England FA stars are in the pictures below?

1

2

3

4

Answers on Page 61

PAUL GASCOIGNE
(v Scotland, Euro 1996, group stage)

This was the goal that kick-started England's Euro '96 campaign after a stalemate with Switzerland and saw Paul Gascoigne controversially make a point to the English press.

England were in front against the auld enemy thanks to Alan Shearer's header but were hanging on grimly in the moments before the goal, and looked to be on the verge of another disappointing result when Scotland were awarded a 77th-minute penalty.

But David Seaman saved Gary McAllister's spot kick and when Scotland conceded a foul from the resulting corner, within seconds it was Gascoigne taking centre stage. Seaman fired the free kick towards the left wing, by which time Gascoigne was running towards the Scotland penalty area.

He was spotted by Darren Anderton, who lobbed the ball forward. Gascoigne met it on the edge of the box, flicked the ball over Colin Hendry with his left foot, ran around him as the defender stumbled and volleyed past Andy Goram with his right.

The Wembley crowd were in raptures and Gascoigne knew exactly how he was going to celebrate the goal that would give England a 2-0 win.

Prior to the tournament, a picture of Gascoigne and teammates indulging in the so-called "dentist's chair" drinking game on a night out in Hong Kong had featured in the British newspapers.

Angry at the criticism sparked by the picture, Gascoigne decided to recreate the pose, lying on his back next to the Scotland goal as teammates squirted liquid from energy drink bottles into his open mouth.

The momentum generated by Gascoigne's brilliance carried England to their famous 4-1 win over Holland in the next game and to the semi-finals where once more Germany and penalties proved their undoing.

Yet, however briefly, England had played in a swashbuckling, fearless fashion epitomised by Gascoigne's second goal. England have not come as close to winning a major tournament since, nor have they played in such an eye-catching fashion as that overseen by Terry Venables.

For Gascoigne, the goal meant a lot for other reasons. At that time playing in Scotland for Rangers, he had overcome two serious injuries which had checked his international career. He ruptured cruciate ligaments in the 1991 FA Cup Final while playing for Tottenham, which meant he missed 21 England games, and broke his leg in 1994, ruling him out for another 15 months.

A Tribute to **STEVEN GERRARD**

Steven Gerrard announced his retirement from international football shortly after returning from Brazil 2014, bringing to an end 14 years of service to his country, during which he won 114 caps, a total bettered only by Peter Shilton and David Beckham.

A dynamic, lung-bursting midfielder for much of his career, he won his first senior England cap against Ukraine in May 2000, a day after his 20th birthday, and picked a famous occasion to bag his first international goal – scoring in England's 5-1 rout of Germany in Munich in 2001.

He went on to score 21 international goals and represent the Three Lions at six major tournaments.

He made his England debut when Kevin Keegan picked him in his squad for Euro 2000. He appeared too in the European Championship Finals in Portugal in 2004 and Ukraine and Poland in 2012.

Though he missed the 2002 World Cup through injury, he played in Germany 2006 and was captain for both South Africa 2010 and Brazil 2014.

He reached the Quarter-Finals at Euro 2004 and in the 2006 World Cup, where England lost to Portugal on each occasion, but set such high standards for himself that, despite being one of only eight players to make more than 100 appearances, he never considered himself an England great.

"In football the hero and legend status is given out far too easily for my liking," he said, before winning his 100th cap against Sweden in November 2012. "As far as playing for England goes, there are only 11 real heroes over history. The rest haven't really delivered, for me."

Main Pic: Gerrard celebrates his goal v Poland, 2013 (which clinched England's place at Brazil 2014); **Left:** His 100th cap v Sweden; **Above:** May 2000 debut.

Nonetheless, there were many memorable moments in an England shirt. Apart from his stunning 30-yard strike in the thrashing of Germany in that World Cup qualifier in Munich, his outstanding individual display in England's 5-1 defeat of Croatia at Wembley in 2009, two superb goals in a 2-1 win over Hungary at Wembley in 2010 that lifted England's spirits after the disappointment of South Africa and the goal against Poland at Wembley in October 2013 that sealed England's place in Brazil are among those that quickly come to mind.

Top left: May 2000 debut; **Top right:** Goal v Germany in Munich, 2001; **Above:** Flying header v Turkey, 2003; **Left:** Scoring v Switzerland, Euro 2004.

Gerrard's club career with Liverpool has seen him win every honour apart from one and he enjoys the unique distinction of being the only player to have scored in the Finals of the FA Cup, League Cup, Uefa Cup and Champions League.

He almost completed the set last year when Liverpool just missed out to Manchester City in the race for the Premier League crown.

England manager Roy Hodgson paid his own tribute, describing Gerrard as "an incredible man and a fantastic footballer, a tremendous captain and an exceptional role model for everyone fortunate to come into contact with him."

Top: v Croatia, Wembley 2009; **Right & below:** 1st Goal v Hungary, 2010.

an incredible man and a fantastic footballer, a tremendous captain and an exceptional role model for everyone fortunate to come into contact with him

Roy Hodgson

Above: 100th cap v Sweden 2012; **Left:** Gerrard celebrates his goal v Poland, 2013 (which clinched England's place at Brazil 2014).

ENGLAND WOMEN

After the excitement of Brazil 2014, stand by for Canada 2015 as England's Women head for their own World Cup Finals, which will be staged between 6 June and 5 July at six venues across the North American country.

The Finals are expanded from 16 to 24 nations for the first time, with England among eight qualifiers from Europe looking to win through to the Final in Vancouver.

England enjoyed an outstanding qualification campaign, including a 9-0 thrashing of Montenegro at the Amex Stadium in Brighton in April in Mark Sampson's first home fixture since taking over as head coach.

Sampson succeeded Hope Powell in the role in December 2013 after Brent Hills had guided the side through the early World Cup qualification rounds. The 32-year-old Welshman had previously been manager of Swansea City's Centre of Excellence and coached Bristol Academy Women to two Women's FA Cup Finals and a second-place finish in the FA Women's Super League.

Casey Stoney

Mark Sampson

Hills has since been appointed Head of Women's Elite Development by The FA with former England striker Marieanne Spacey brought in as Sampson's assistant.

The victory over Montenegro, in which Manchester City striker Toni Duggan scored a hat-trick, was the biggest by an England Women's team since a 13-0 win over Hungary in a World Cup qualifier in 2005 and came during a run of seven matches in the 2015 qualifying campaign in which the side took maximum points without conceding a goal.

Ukraine were the first team to score against England but it did not detract from a hard-fought 2-1 win in Lviv in June that put Sampson's team on the brink of securing their place in the Finals after former captain Casey Stoney, the Arsenal defender, headed the 11th-minute opener and Chelsea striker Eniola Aluko scored a second three minutes later, her ninth goal of the campaign.

Steph Houghton

Toni Duggan

Fara Williams

The match saw Fara Williams, the Liverpool midfielder, equal Arsenal winger Rachel Yankey's record of 129 international caps.

Stoney, 32, was succeeded as captain in April by 26-year-old Manchester City defender Steph Houghton, who is expected to lead the side as they look to achieve their best-ever World Cup performance in Canada, having previously reached the quarter-finals on three occasions.

Eniola Aluko

QUIZ TIME!
20 QUESTIONS

Think you know everything about the England squad? Think again...

1. Who was the only member of England's 2014 World Cup squad not attached to a club in the Barclay's Premier League?

2. Which England striker scored six goals at the 1986 World Cup Finals in Mexico?

3. Which member of England's squad at the 2014 World Cup Finals began his career with Shrewsbury Town?

4. Who scored his first England goal against Macedonia in September 2003 aged 17 years and 317 days?

5. Which club side did former England manager Bobby Robson and former captain Bryan Robson both play for?

6. Which outfield player holds the record for the most England appearances without scoring a goal?

7. Why does Jermain Defoe appear in England's record books next to the number 34?

8. What happened when England visited Munich on September 1, 2001?

9. Which defender appeared for England in 15 consecutive seasons between 1997 and 2011?

10. Which Watford player made 31 England appearances between May 1983 and May 1987?

11. Which player won 36 England caps while playing for Real Madrid?

12. Which England player scored 19 of his 27 international goals while playing for clubs in Italy?

13. Which England midfield player missed a penalty in a World Cup penalty shoot-out and was sent off in his final international appearance?

14. Which team inflicted England's heaviest defeat in May 1954?

15. Which England record does striker Peter Crouch share with goalkeeper Fraser Forster?

16. What does Alex Oxlade-Chamberlain have in common with Shaun Wright-Phillips, Frank Lampard and Nigel Clough?

17. Goalkeeper Peter Shilton earned 83 of his 125 international caps under which England manager?

18. Which team did England beat at the quarter-final stage of the 1990 World Cup Finals in Italy?

19. Which England manager resigned after England lost to Germany in the last match played at the old Wembley stadium?

20. In which World Cup Finals were England eliminated without losing one of their five matches and conceding only one goal?

Answers on Page 61

ENGLAND'S GREATEST GOALS #4

MICHAEL OWEN
(v Argentina, World Cup France 1998, round of 16)

There were some who questioned Glenn Hoddle's wisdom in trusting the raw teenage talent of Michael Owen with a place in his World Cup squad in France in 1998.

Not many did after he provided fans with a goal so brilliant, so unexpected and so fearless it was almost frozen in time.

St Etienne, France: England v Argentina, the last 16 of the World Cup. For England fans the occasion was dominated by talk of revenge, for the defeat inflicted by Diego Maradona's 'hand of God' in 1986.

England's team, toughened by the experience of Paul Ince, Tony Adams and Alan Shearer, had performed well to escape a group containing Colombia, Tunisia and Romania. Liverpool striker Owen had made substitute appearances but started England's final game with Colombia and did well enough to keep his place.

Against Argentina, only 16 minutes into an eventful match already 1-1 after a penalty for each side, a chipped pass from David Beckham was skilfully brought under control by Owen in the centre circle, flicking the ball forward as he turned.

Instinctively, quite unfazed by the occasion, the teenager charged at the Argentine defence; they never stood a chance of catching him.

He shrugged off the challenge of one defender, jinked to the right to sidestep another before slamming the ball into the opposite corner, making the score 2-1 in the blink of an eye and bringing a nation to its feet.

It is a measure of what a memorable goal it was that its place in folklore was secure despite England suffering yet another painful defeat that night in France, again on penalties.

A clever free-kick routine saw Argentina equalise through Javier Zanetti just before half-time. Then just after the break, Beckham left his teammates facing an uphill task by being sent off for petulantly kicking out at Diego Simeone as he was lying on the floor.

England fought manfully and defender Sol Campbell could yet have salvaged a quarter-final berth, only for his header to be ruled out after the referee spotted a push.

Faced with another penalty shoot-out, England once more were found wanting from 12 yards as Ince and substitute David Batty missed their kicks.

Argentina progressed, yet the distraught England fans filing out of the Stade Geoffroy-Guichard that night would always have 'that goal' from Owen to cherish.

MIDFIELDERS

Ross **Barkley**

Born: Liverpool, 5 December, 1993

Ross Barkley emerged as England's great hope going into last summer's World Cup and Everton fans will be anxious to see his precocious talents stay on Merseyside for longer than another brilliant teenager, Wayne Rooney.

Born in the Liverpool suburb of Wavertree, Barkley broke through at Goodison Park last season, scoring on the opening day against Norwich before attracting acclaim for his displays against Arsenal and Swansea.

Barkley made his first senior appearance for Everton in 2011 against Queen's Park Rangers in a debut that might have come sooner but for a broken leg sustained on England under-19 duty. He developed his game in loan spells at Sheffield Wednesday and Leeds in the 2012-13 season, scoring four times for the Hillsborough club.

The 6ft 2in midfielder, another who enjoys the No 10 role behind the forwards, joined Everton's academy as an 11-year-old in 2005.

He has represented his country at five different age groups and won his first senior cap aged 19 in a World Cup qualifier against Moldova in August 2013. He featured heavily in England's warm-up games for last summer's World Cup, making his first international start against Ecuador, and he appeared in all three matches at the Finals, with a place in the starting line-up for the final group game against Costa Rica.

DID YOU KNOW

Before he committed himself to playing for England, Ross remained eligible to represent Nigeria in international football because he has a Nigerian grandfather.

Tom **Cleverley**

Born: Basingstoke, Hampshire, 12 August, 1989

Manchester United's Tom Cleverley has the energy and quality on the ball to challenge for a key role in England's midfield following the retirement of Frank Lampard and Steven Gerrard.

He made 31 appearances for United in the 2013-14 season before moving to Aston Villa on a season-long loan to further his development as a Premier League player.

The dynamic central midfielder made 16 appearances for the Under-21s, also starring for Team GB at the 2012 Olympics. After featuring in two of Fabio Capello's squads, Cleverley won his first cap in August 2012 against Italy in Berne and started several of England's qualifiers for last summer's Finals in Brazil before falling down the pecking order.

Cleverly joined United from Bradford City as a schoolboy, and shone in loan spells with Leicester City, Watford and Wigan Athletic, for whom he scored the first Premier League goal of his career for Wigan in an away defeat to West Ham United in November 2010

Sir Alex Ferguson made Cleverley a fixture of his first-team squad at the start of the 2011-12 campaign, with the midfielder making his senior debut against Manchester City in the Community Shield, before he played a pivotal role in United's 8-2 thrashing of Arsenal in August 2011. He scored his first United goal in a 2-1 League Cup win over Newcastle United in September 2012.

DID YOU KNOW?

Tom's winners' medal for his part in Manchester United's 2012-13 title triumph in Sir Alex Ferguson's final year in charge was not his first – he made enough appearances in a loan spell at Leicester City to earn one for their 2008-09 League One championship success.

Jordan **Henderson**

Born: Sunderland, 17 June, 1990

Reportedly worth £20m to Liverpool when they bought him from Sunderland in 2011, Jordan Henderson has overcome the close scrutiny that goes with a high-value transfer to help the Anfield club return to the Champions League and win himself the possibility of a long-term future in England's midfield.

Henderson came through the ranks on Wearside and became a fixture of Sunderland's starting line-up aged just 19, after impressing in a loan spell at Coventry City the previous season, in which he bagged his first senior goal against Norwich.

In two full seasons at the Stadium of Light, Henderson excelled wherever he was deployed, be it in his preferred position as a holding central midfielder or on the right wing, and he won Sunderland's Young Player of the Year award in 2010 and 2011.

In his time at Anfield he has always been a regular, but only fully justified his price tag during the 2013-14 season, where his mature and increasingly attacking performances saw manager Brendan Rodgers describe him as the Premier League's 'most improved player'.

Henderson won 27 under-21 caps and was the team's Player of the Year for 2012, going on to captain the side at the 2013 under-21 European Championships. A year on, he started England's World Cup in Brazil as a first-choice pick having become a regular member of Roy Hodgson's squad in friendlies prior to the tournament.

DID YOU KNOW?

Jordan won his first England cap under the management of Fabio Capello in a friendly against France in 2010 but had to wait 18 months for the second, in a warm-up match for Euro 2012 against Norway.

Adam **Lallana**

Born: St Albans, Herts, 10 May, 1988

Attacking midfielder Adam Lallana was plying his trade in League One as recently as 2011 but had become a player England fans were clamouring to be picked when last summer's World Cup kicked off in Brazil.

His form, which helped inspire the Saints to eighth place in the Premier League in 2013-14 having won promotion from the third tier only three years earlier, prompted Liverpool to spend £25m to end his 14 year association with the Hampshire club.

Lallana has enjoyed most success deployed in a number 10 role, where his ability on the ball and superb close control saw him score 12 Premier League goals in two seasons for Southampton, while forging a formidable partnership with striker Rickie Lambert, who also moved to Anfield last summer.

The midfielder made his senior debut for Southampton in 2006, in a League Cup tie with Yeovil, and spent a brief period on loan at Bournemouth, whose Centre of Excellence he had been attending when Saints scouts first spotted him.

Lallana passed under the radar to such an extent as a youngster that his tally of senior caps has already overtaken the number of appearances he made for England's under-18, under-19 and under-21 sides, for whom he played once each before making his senior debut against Chile at Wembley in November, 2013. His performances in friendlies earned him a berth in Roy Hodgson's World Cup squad and he made his competitive international debut as a substitute in England's opening match with Italy.

DID YOU KNOW

Apart from his humble football beginnings, Adam has also overcome health problems to forge a career at the highest level. He was diagnosed with an irregular heartbeat when he was only 18 and had to undergo surgery to correct it.

James **Milner**

Born: Leeds, 4 January, 1986

Few people grudge hard-working James Milner the major honours that have come his way at Manchester City; now the Yorkshireman hopes to add an international medal as he enters the peak of his career.

Since moving to the Etihad Stadium in 2010 in a move that reportedly valued him at around £20 million, Milner has won all three major domestic trophies, including two Premier League titles, and the combative midfielder had proved reliable in many positions under Roberto Mancini and Manuel Pellegrini. This flexibility was underlined by Roy Hodgson experimenting by playing Milner at right back in a warm-up match for last summer's World Cup.

Milner began at hometown club Leeds United, having been a ball boy and season ticket holder at Elland Road before joining as a player, but was forced to leave for Newcastle in 2004 owing to Leeds' financial difficulties. A mixed spell in the North East preceded a move to Aston Villa in 2008, following a loan spell in Birmingham two years before.

At Villa, he flourished under the tutelage of Martin O'Neill, producing such dynamic performances he was awarded his senior England debut in 2009 and a place in the 2010 World Cup squad. In winning his 47th senior cap against Ecuador before last year's Finals, Milner overtook his tally of 46 appearances for England's under-21s, which is a national record.

Milner started all England's matches at Euro 2012 but played only in the match against Costa Rica in Brazil last summer, by which time England's fate was already determined. He scored his first international goal in England's crushing 5-0 World Cup qualification win in Moldova in September 2012.

DID YOU KNOW?

James's winning goal for Leeds at Sunderland on Boxing Day, 2002 saw him become the Premier League's youngest ever scorer at the age of 16 years and 356 days. The man whose record he eclipsed was England teammate Wayne Rooney.

Alex **Oxlade-Chamberlain**

Born: Portsmouth, 15 August, 1993

Affectionately known as the Ox to fans of Arsenal and England, Alex-Oxlade-Chamberlain threatened to be a leading light for the national side at the World Cup only for injury to rule him out of England's three group games in Brazil.

Arsene Wenger will not have been surprised by how much Oxlade-Chamberlain's absence at the World Cup was a blow to England, having spent £15m including add-ons on the attacking midfielder when he was a teenage prospect at Southampton.

Oxlade-Chamberlain scored four goals in eight appearances for the Under-21s but had won only one cap for the senior team, in a warm-up match, before starting England's opening clash with France in Euro 2012. Oxlade-Chamberlain scored his first international goal against San Marino in September 2012, doubling his tally for England against the same opposition six months later.

Born in Portsmouth, where his father Mark played between 1988 and 1994, Oxlade-Chamberlain began his career at Pompey's bitter rivals Southampton, as an academy graduate, and helped the Saints win promotion from League One to the Championship in 2011.

Oxlade-Chamberlain has helped Arsenal secure top-four finishes in each of his three years at the club, but injury meant he made only 14 Premier League appearances in the 2013-14 season and he missed The FA Cup Final.

DID YOU KNOW?

Before opting for football, Alex was offered a trial with rugby union club London Irish and become the youngest centurion in Hampshire League cricket when he made 100 not out for Locks Heath aged 13.

Fabian **Delph'**

Born: Bradford, 21 November, 1989

Aston Villa midfielder, Fabian Delph, earned a call-up to the senior England squad for last September's friendly international against Norway at Wembley, ahead of the opening Euro 2016 qualifier against Switzerland in Basel.

The 25-year-old, a former England Under-21 international, established himself as a regular member of Aston Villa's Premier League side towards the end of the 2012-13 season and enjoyed an excellent 2013-14 campaign, when he was regarded as one of the most consistent performers in Paul Lambert's side.

Delph was on the books of Bradford City as a youngster before moving to Leeds United as an 11 year old. After signing on scholarship terms as a 16 year old, he made his Leeds debut, aged 17, at the end of the 2006-07 season and made such quick progress that he was soon attracting a big following of Premier League scouts to Elland Road.

Most of his experience for Leeds came at League One level but Villa were impressed with his potential and Leeds accepted an offer of around £6 million to let him move to Villa Park in August 2009.

His progress with the Midlands side was interrupted by a cruciate ligament injury in April 2010 that kept him out for the next eight months and he was hampered by an ankle injury after returning to Leeds on loan in January 2012. But he has worked hard to improve his overall fitness after recovering from that setback and his outstanding form in 2013-14, which included a first Premier League goal in a win at Southampton, was his reward.

DID YOU KNOW?

Fabian could have represented Guyana in international football had he not committed himself to England.

Andros **Townsend**

Born: Leytonstone, London, 16 July, 1991

Few players enjoyed a more eye-catching role in England winning a place at the 2014 World Cup Finals than Tottenham midfielder Andros Townsend and it was unlucky for him that injury deprived him of the opportunity to travel to Brazil.

The former Leyton Orient midfielder is noted for his fearless attacking instincts as he relentlessly storms past defenders before whipping in crosses or shooting from distance.

There was understandable enthusiasm among England fans as Townsend managed to show off these traits at the top level, scoring on his senior debut in October, 2013, in a crucial 4-1 Wembley win over Montenegro.

That victory and the subsequent 2-0 win over Poland, in which Townsend was also key, helped England qualify for the Brazil Finals but then came the setback of an ankle ligament injury suffered in action for Tottenham in April, which meant Roy Hodgson had to rule him out of his plans for Brazil.

Townsend's England emergence also coincided with a breakthrough at White Hart Lane after several spells on loan with other clubs, although a change of manager at Tottenham and his subsequent injury somewhat checked his progress.

DID YOU KNOW?

Andros has been on the senior books at Tottenham only since 2009 yet has made 110 appearances for nine different loan clubs in that period.

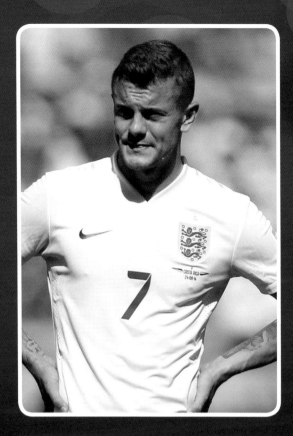

Jack **Wilshere**

Born: Stevenage, Hertfordshire, 1 January, 1992

Hugely talented Arsenal midfielder Jack Wilshere has seen his progress checked by a spate of injury problems but was fit enough to travel to the World Cup in Brazil last summer after helping the Gunners end their nine-year trophy drought.

The central midfielder's development as a teenager was so rapid he had almost become an automatic pick for England before a broken ankle meant he missed the whole of the 2011-12 Premier League season and the European Championship in Poland and Ukraine.

Wilshere first impressed in Arsene Wenger's youthful Carling Cup teams, before making his Premier League breakthrough in a loan spell at Bolton Wanderers. He returned to North London for the 2010-11 season and had a sensational year, attracting praise across Europe for his performance in Arsenal's 2-1 Champions League win over Barcelona.

Wilshere is a complete international midfielder with a tough tackle, good close control, a deceptive turn of pace and a superb passing range. When fit, he has been a fixture in Arsenal's midfield and England squads since 2012, but he has continued to suffer injury problems. Over the summer of 2013, he underwent minor ankle surgery and missed six weeks towards the end of the 2013-14 campaign when he sustained a hairline fracture to the foot. He returned to fitness in time to appear in The FA Cup Final with Hull as a substitute.

Wilshere won his first senior cap – as a substitute against Hungary in August 2010 – when just 18 years old and frequently featured in England's qualification for the World Cup before making two substitute appearances at the Finals in Brazil.

DID YOU KNOW?

Jack spent a brief period in the youth academy at Luton Town before being plucked from there by eagle-eyed Arsenal coaches when he was just nine years old.

...and farewell to
Frank **Lampard**

Frank Lampard followed Steven Gerrard in announcing his retirement from international football following the 2014 World Cup finals in Brazil, having captained the side in England's closing match against Costa Rica.

Roy Hodgson's decision to give Lampard the captain's armband was recognition of his contribution to the national team in a career that saw him win 106 caps and play in the finals of three major tournaments.

He put in some of his best performances in the 2004 European Championship finals in Portugal, where he scored three goals in England's run to the quarter-finals. He also hit five goals in the qualifying campaign for the 2006 World Cup, including the 80th-minute strike against Poland that secured qualification.

In total he scored 29 international goals, although he will be remembered too for one he was famously denied against Germany in the last 16 of the 2010 World Cup finals in South Africa, when the officials wrongly judged his shot to have not crossed the line after hitting the underside of the bar.

A Champions League, Europa League and three-times Premier League champion, Lampard left Chelsea at the end of the 2013-14 season after 648 appearances and 211 goals for the Stamford Bridge club.

He called time on his years in London in order to join the new Major League Soccer team New York City, although he continued his career in the Premier League with a loan move to Manchester City.

His defining triumph in club football came in May 2012 when Chelsea beat Bayern Munich on penalties – with Lampard captaining the side – to win the Champions League, which came after three semi-final exits and a painful penalty shoot-out loss to Manchester United in the 2008 final.

Lampard was a brilliant young player at West Ham United — under the management of his uncle, Harry Redknapp — before Claudio Ranieri spent £11m to take him to Chelsea in 2003. In West London, Lampard became a club legend, overtaking Bobby Tambling as the club's all-time leading scorer last year.

He won his first senior international cap while with the Hammers, in a 1999 friendly win over Belgium. He finishes level with Sir Bobby Charlton as the sixth most-capped player in England history.

Back in the day: 1975

This was the year memorable for the high spots of what would be a brief but explosive England career for the prolific goalscorer Malcolm Macdonald, whose exploits made him a fans' favourite at Luton, Arsenal and Newcastle. In 359 League games for the three clubs combined, 'Supermac' scored 186 goals.

Macdonald made his England debut in 1972 but had to wait almost three years and seven more caps to score his first goal, England's second in a 2-0 win over West Germany in a friendly at Wembley, when the World Cup holders provided the opposition for England's 100th international fixture.

His finest night in an England shirt came a month later, when the muscular centre forward scored all five goals in a 5-0 demolition of Cyprus in a European Championship qualifier, becoming the first player to score five in one match at Wembley. Yet despite this history-making exhibition of forward play it would be his last appearance for the national side at Wembley.

England's year under Don Revie's management went well until the moment when it mattered. In the Home Internationals, a goalless draw against Northern Ireland equalled England's record of six consecutive clean sheets, Ipswich forward David Johnson scored twice on his debut against Wales and superb performances from Alan Ball, Colin Bell and Gerry Francis tore apart Scotland in a 5-1 Wembley romp.

But Revie dropped Ball in the autumn and England's bid to qualify for the 1976 European Championship collapsed with a 2-1 defeat to Czechoslovakia in Bratislava, followed by a 1-1 draw against Portugal in Lisbon. The Czechs, needing only a draw, beat Cyprus in their last qualification match to eliminate England.

Malcolm Macdonald

Colin Bell

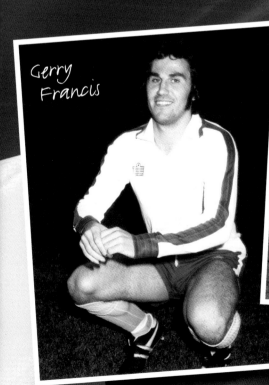

Gerry Francis

QUIZ TIME!
WORDSEARCH

Can you find all 18 player surnames in the grid below? Words can go horizontally, vertically and diagonally in all eight directions.

```
N C N B T B G V J V P N K S L
O H O G T Z E O K T N U H T W
S R S F Y P H C Z R L R W E R
P L R T B N G Z N S M J K R R
M M E R S W L R Z E N N E L G
O T D O E H G H P N M H D I J
H K N B U D C D H R G E C N P
T Y E G R U K L L A P C L G K
N O H Z O F Q N R B B Z P C E
R E W R G E R R A R D K P W E
S E C E L Y A D N P M F R M G
V X L A N C V V V R P Y V N A
Q L E W S T U R R I D G E R N
Q N V T O F N A M A N A M C M
G L R T Z F G K H F R N F B Z
```

Barnes	Crouch	Henderson	Johnson	Neal	Sterling
Carragher	Fowler	Hughes	Keegan	Owen	Sturridge
Clemence	Gerrard	Hunt	McManaman	Redknapp	Thompson

Answers on Page 61

ENGLAND'S GREATEST GOALS #5

DAVID BECKHAM
(v Greece, World Cup qualifier, 2001)

All will be cherished but this one, for its drama and multiple subtexts, was more special than most.

David Beckham, England's captain, capped a talismanic performance at Old Trafford on October 6, 2001, by curling home one of his trademark free-kicks in the 93rd minute to seal a 2-2 draw and with it qualification for the 2002 Finals in Japan and South Korea.

Greece had lost their other three away games, including a 5-1 loss to Finland, so for England to stumble against them with only a point needed to qualify would have been a bitter pill to swallow. Yet Beckham had to drag a nervous England through the match almost single-handedly, seeming to cover almost every blade of grass on the pitch.

The euphoria and relief inside Old Trafford was all the more sweet for the fact that the nation Beckham consigned to the play-offs with his stunning late goal was Germany, beaten in 1966 but England's bête-noire almost ever since, the architects their Semi-Final defeats at Italia '90 and Euro '96.

In one of the highlights of Sven-Goran Eriksson's term as manager, England had spectacularly dispatched Germany 5-1 in Munich only a month before this match with Greece. Yet the thrill of that victory at the Olympiastadion would have been forever tarnished if England had let it go to waste. Instead it was Germany who were subjected to a two-legged play-off with Ukraine.

For Beckham, the moment of brilliance turned his personal fortunes full circle after the disappointment of his red card at France '98, and his joyful celebrations left no one in any doubt that to score a goal of such importance meant a lot to him, fulfilling his desire to perform great deeds in an England shirt as he had so many times in his club career.

Players more talented than Beckham have scored goals just as eye-catching as this one, good though it was. But it followed a display of courage and fortitude of the highest order, capped by having the nerve to deliver when failure would not only have lost the match but let down the nation. This time Beckham was the hero, and deservedly so.

STRIKERS

Jermain **Defoe**

Born: Beckton, London, 7 October, 1982

Described as one of the most natural finishers of his generation, Jermain Defoe said goodbye to Tottenham in 2014, having made the move across the Atlantic to play in Major League Soccer for Toronto. But he remained in Roy Hodgson's thoughts, making the standby list for the World Cup Finals.

Despite having been to two World Cups with England and boasting a career goals tally in excess of 200, major honours at international and club level have eluded Defoe. Tottenham won the League Cup in 2008 shortly after he left the club to join Portsmouth, and while the Hampshire club won The FA Cup in the same year Defoe did not get a medal as he was cup-tied.

His international high spots have included the goal against Slovenia that took England into the last 16 at the 2010 World Cup Finals and a hat-trick in a Euro 2012 qualifier against Bulgaria at Wembley. He marked his 50th cap with a goal in England's 5-0 win in Moldova in September 2012.

Small in stature but blessed with pace, the forward first came to prominence during a loan spell at Bournemouth in 2000-01, where he scored in 10 consecutive matches during a prolific run of scoring 18 goals in 29 league games.

He became a favourite at parent club West Ham, displaying his poacher instincts in scoring 41 goals for the East London club before being tempted into a move to Tottenham six months after the Hammers lost their Premier league status in 2003. A fans favourite at White Hart Lane, he scored his 100th goal for Tottenham in 2011.

DID YOU KNOW?

Jermain has played at three different clubs under Harry Redknapp, who was his manager at West Ham, took him from Tottenham to Portsmouth and then back to Spurs in 2009.

Rickie **Lambert**

Born: Kirkby, Merseyside, 16 February, 1982

A long journey taking in the less-than-glamorous surroundings of Macclesfield, Stockport and Rochdale has taken Rickie Lambert from being a Liverpool academy reject in 1997 to a return to Anfield in a £4m move last summer.

The 32-year-old striker's rise back up the ranks was completed in a prolific five-year spell at Southampton, where his 117 goals in 235 appearances for the Saints helped the Hampshire club move from League One in 2011 to a top-ten Premier League finish last year.

After receiving his first England call-up at the age of 31, Lambert scored with his first touch in international football, towering above defenders in trademark fashion to head in the winner in a 3-2 victory over Scotland at Wembley in August 2013.

He also netted in a vital qualifying win for England against Moldova a month later and was named in Roy Hodgson's 23-man squad for the tournament in Brazil, making his first appearance in the competition as a substitute against Uruguay.

After a mixed scoring record in spells at Macclesfield Town and Stockport County between 2000 and 2005, the 6ft 2in Lambert's breakthrough season came with Bristol Rovers in 2008-09 when he scored 29 league goals for the Pirates.

DID YOU KNOW?

Rickie's third child, Bella Rose, was born on August 8, 2013, the same day the proud dad received his first call-up to the England squad.

Wayne **Rooney**

Born: Croxteth, Liverpool, 24 October, 1985

England Captain, Wayne Rooney, remains a key member of the England side as he prepares to turn 30 and has been since he dramatically announced himself on the international stage at Euro 2004 by scoring four goals.

Five times a Premier League champion, Rooney won his first senior cap against Australia at the age of 17 in 2003, and seems almost certain to join the esteemed list of players capped 100 times after his participation in the World Cup Finals in Brazil took his total appearances into the 90s.

Rooney broke his World Cup goal duck by scoring England's equaliser against Uruguay but could not inspire his country to glory at the Finals. Italy, who also beat England in Brazil, foiled Rooney at Euro 2012 after the Liverpudlian returned from suspension to score the winner for England against Ukraine in their final group game.

After embarking upon his professional career under David Moyes at Everton, Rooney secured a lucrative move to Manchester United in 2004 and, aside from The FA Cup, has won every major trophy in his time at Old Trafford, including the Champions League in 2008. He scored at Wembley in the 2011 Final of that competition, which United ultimately lost 3-1 to Barcelona.

The dynamic forward – who has been deployed in central midfield as he has matured at United – made his senior debut for Everton aged 16. He has scored more than 200 goals for United, reaching that landmark against Bayer Leverkusen in September 2013.

DID YOU KNOW?

Raheem **Sterling**

Born: Kingston, Jamaica, 8 December, 1994

Raheem Sterling lifted England fans to their feet with his dynamic and fearless performance against Italy at last summer's World Cup and has an opportunity to feature prominently for England for years to come.

Having almost won a Premier League title as a teenager after helping Liverpool go agonisingly close to ending their 25-year wait to regain the championship, Sterling seems certain to win major honours in the years to come.

A Queens Park Rangers player until 2010, Sterling made his senior debut for Liverpool against Wigan in March 2012, becoming the second youngest player in the club's history.

He scored his first goal for Liverpool against Reading in October, 2012 and featured prominently in Brendan Rodgers' first season in charge before blossoming during the 2013-14 campaign, in which he scored nine times in 30 Premier League appearances.

Sterling made several appearances for England's under-16, under-17, under-19 and under-21 sides, before earning a debut for the senior team against Sweden in November, 2012. He established his place as a squad regular in warm-up games for the World Cup last summer and, despite a red card in a pre-tournament clash with Ecuador in Miami, Sterling emerged from England's group games at the Finals with credit.

DID YOU KNOW?

Raheem was born in Jamaica but moved to London aged five, growing up within just a few yards of Wembley Stadium.

Daniel **Sturridge**

Born: Birmingham, 1 September, 1989

One half of the deadly Anfield strike partnership known as 'SaS', Daniel Sturridge was England's preferred number nine at the World Cup last summer and showed the ability that brought him 21 Premier League goals for Liverpool last season by netting in England's opening game with Italy.

The winger-cum-forward, who endured less fulfilling times at Manchester City and Chelsea before thriving alongside Luis Suarez at Anfield, scored a typically stylish left-footed strike in a World Cup warm-up win over Peru last summer and seems set to feature for England up front for many years to come.

Sturridge was held in high regard at City – winning the club's Young Player of the Year award for 2008-09 – but left for Chelsea in July 2009, where he appeared only sporadically at first.

A loan spell at Bolton in 2011 – in which he scored eight times in 12 games – persuaded Andre Villas-Boas to make Sturridge an integral part of his plans at Stamford Bridge and he helped the London side win the FA Cup and Champions League glory in 2012, scoring 13 goals along the way.

His performances gained him senior international recognition for the first time, winning his debut cap against Sweden at Wembley in November 2011, and he was picked in Stuart Pearce's squad for the London 2012 Olympics after being overlooked for Euro 2012.

DID YOU KNOW?

Daniel was born in Birmingham City Hospital, where his former Manchester City teammate Micah Richards was delivered 15 months earlier.

Danny **Welbeck**

Born: Longsight, Manchester, 26 November, 1990

Fast and athletic, Danny Welbeck has been lucky to learn from two world-class colleagues in Robin Van Persie and Wayne Rooney at Manchester United, becoming one of the Premier League's most adaptable and dependable forwards in his own right before signing for Arsenal on transfer deadline day last summer.

Welbeck, whose parents are both Ghanaian, rose to international prominence at Euro 2012, and produced the inspired backheel to nab England a critical winner in their 3-2 victory over Sweden in the group stages. He won his first senior cap against his parents' native country Ghana in 2011.

The Manchester-born striker has scored goals at five different levels for England, starting with the under-17s in 2006. Welbeck's goal in England's 1-0 win against Belgium at Wembley in June 2012 was his first international strike.

Welbeck first appeared for United in 2008 before a season-long loan at Sunderland in 2010-11 underlined his potential – the forward scored his first goal of six for the Wearsiders in a memorable 3-0 win at Chelsea.

On returning to Old Trafford, he became an established regular and a Premier League champion in 2012-13. Welbeck can play in wide midfield and as a lone striker, and is proficient at holding the ball up and bringing his strike partner or midfield teammates into play.

DID YOU KNOW?

Born in Longsight, Danny had a trial with Manchester City at the age of eight before joining United.

England's **Under-21s**

England's Under-21s head coach Gareth Southgate believes he has a group of players capable of competing at the highest level after a successful first season in the role.

Nathan Redmond

The former England defender's Under-21 team finished top of their qualifying group for the 2015 European Under-21 championship Finals in Czechoslovakia, giving them the chance to reach the Finals via a two-legged play-off.

He was encouraged in particular after he took an Under-20s team to compete in the Toulon Under-21 Tournament in France in 2014, where they finished fourth after playing five matches in just 11 days. Their only defeat in the group stage came against a strong, physical Brazil Under-21 side and they were a little unlucky to lose to Portugal in a play-off for third and fourth place.

The majority of that squad will be able to feature in next summer's Finals and there was valuable tournament experience for nine players who had never featured for the Under-21s before.

Jack Butland

Nonetheless, the England side that faced Portugal included five players with Barclays Premier League experience in goalkeeper Jack Butland, James Ward-Prowse, Nathan Redmond, Saido Berahino and Cauley Woodrow, plus five who had played in the Sky Bet Championship in Ben Gibson, Liam Moore, Nathaniel Chalobah, Jake Foster-Caskey and Will Keane.

Ward-Prowse showed his dead-ball prowess by scoring with a superbly hit free kick against Brazil, who had to withstand a strong second-half showing from England to secure a 2-1 win. Brazil won all their group games, culminating in a 7-0 thrashing of Qatar, and defeated France 5-2 in the Final.

There were goals in the group matches too for Woodrow, Foster-Caskey, Jordan Obita and Jordan Cousins.

Established players such as Tom Ince, Wilfried Zaha, Ravel Morrison, Carl Jenkinson, Patrick Bamford and Will Hughes have also featured in Southgate's Under-21 teams.

England last reached the Final of a European Under-21 championships in Sweden in 2009 when they lost 4-0 to a German side that included six members of the squad Joachim Low took to last year's senior World Cup in Brazil, five of whom figured in the side that beat Argentina in the Final.

Liam Moore

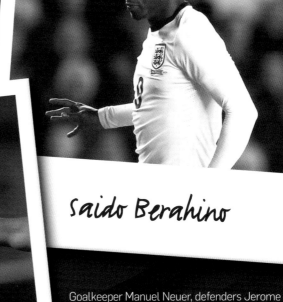

Saido Berahino

Jordan Cousins

Goalkeeper Manuel Neuer, defenders Jerome Boateng, Benedikt Howedes and Mats Hummels, plus midfielders Sami Khedira and Mesut Ozil were part of a formidable German line-up against an England side that included Micah Richards, Kieran Gibbs, Lee Cattermole, James Milner and Theo Walcott.

Back in the day: 1990

Paul Gascoigne

This was a year of what might have been for England. They might have won the World Cup for a second time and in doing so might have avenged the injustice of Diego Maradona's 'Hand of God' goal in 1986...if only their luck had not deserted them at the critical moment.

And they did enjoy some luck. They were far from impressive in drawing 1-1 with Jack Charlton's Republic of Ireland in their opening group match and though Paul Gascoigne produced a performance worthy of the world stage against The Netherlands, again England took only a point and failed to score. Mark Wright's header — the only goal — decided a tense final group game against Egypt, sending England through as group-winners.

But in the last 16, England were heading for a penalty shoot-out against Belgium until David Platt's spectacular swivelling volley 30 seconds from the end of extra time and in the quarter-finals it took two penalties — one seven minutes from the end of normal time and a second in extra time — to get past an adventurous, attacking Cameroon.

England saved their best performance until last, in the semi-final against West Germany, but this time had no luck. Behind to an Andreas Brehme free kick that beat Peter Shilton only because of an enormous deflection off Paul Parker, England deservedly equalised through Gary Lineker 10 minutes from time but in extra time saw a Chris Waddle shot come back off the inside of a post and a Platt header disallowed for offside.

After Gazza's tears at the yellow card that would rule him out of the Final even if England had got there came the wider agony of the penalty shoot-out, with Waddle and Stuart Pearce the two players wishing the ground would open up and swallow them after missing their kicks.

England were out and it was no consolation to them that Brehme said later that they would have won the Final against a cynical Argentina, yet Bobby Robson left the stage with his reputation intact as the most successful England manager since Sir Alf Ramsey. .

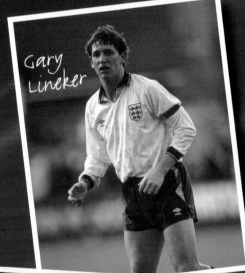

Gary Lineker

Bobby Robson

David Platt

A Tribute to **Sir TOM FINNEY**

It has been said that Sir Tom Finney, who died in 2014 at the age of 91, was the complete footballer, a player who combined technical brilliance with tactical intelligence and sportsmanship.

Comfortable on either wing and later as a deep-lying centre forward, he played in 473 competitive matches for Preston, scoring 210 goals, and won 76 England caps, yet was never booked or sent off in his whole 24-year career.

Finney was also faithfully loyal to one club, Preston North End, staying at Deepdale despite lucrative offers to play abroad, where he could have more than doubled his basic wage and earned as much on top in bonuses.

Bill Shankly, a Preston teammate who would later become a legendary Liverpool manager, reckoned Finney was so good he could have taken on and beaten an opposing full-back "wearing an overcoat." Others have said that had he been a footballer today he would be seen as the equal of Lionel Messi.

The only thing missing from Finney's glittering career was some major silverware. He played in three World Cups and an FA Cup Final but his only medals were for the 1941 Wartime Cup, when Preston beat Arsenal 2-1, and the 1951 Second Division championship.

Finney was born a street away from Deepdale. His childhood health had been poor and when Preston offered him a trial he was only 4ft 9in tall and weighed less than five stone, yet he was offered a contract to join the ground staff. Famously, his father insisted that he first learn a trade, so he signed as an amateur and completed an apprenticeship in plumbing. Nicknamed the Preston Plumber, he returned to the trade once his playing days were over.

War delayed his League debut for Preston until 1946, when he lined up against Leeds United at the age of 24 on opening day of the first post-War season. He made his England debut in a 7-2 trouncing of Northern Ireland in 1946, in which he scored the first of his 30 international goals, which was then a record.

He retired in 1960 – at the end of a season when he had played 43 games, scoring 21 goals. He became president of the club, a magistrate and chairman of his local health authority. In 1998 he was knighted.

QUIZ TIME!
ANSWERS

Crossword, P12

How well did you do?

Maze, P24

Did you solve them all?

Guess Who?, P34

Jack Wilshere

Glen Johnson

Daniel Sturridge

Fraser Forster

Wordsearch, P50

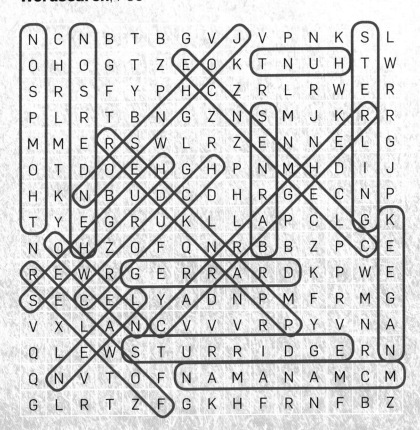

20 Questions, P42

1 Fraser Forster, the Glasgow Celtic goalkeeper.

2 Gary Lineker

3 Joe Hart

4 Wayne Rooney

5 West Bromwich Albion

6 Ashley Cole. 107 games without a goal.

7 That's the number of appearances for England Jermain made as a substitute, more than any other player.

8 England won 5-1 in a World Cup qualifier.

9 Rio Ferdinand.

10 John Barnes.

11 David Beckham.

12 David Platt, who played for Bari, Juventus and Sampdoria.

13 David Batty, who missed a penalty in the shoot-out against Argentina at France '98 and was sent off in his final appearance against Poland in 1999.

14 Hungary beat England 7-1 in Budapest.

15 At 6ft 7ins they share the record as the tallest to play for England.

16 They all followed their fathers Mark Chamberlain, Ian Wright, Frank Lampard senior and Brian Cough in playing for England.

17 Bobby Robson.

18 Cameroon.

19 Kevin Keegan.

20 Spain 1982, when Ron Greenwood's side won all three of their matches in the first group stage but went out after drawing both in the second group stage.